D0117897

gaudíguide

Editorial Gustavo Gili, SA

08029 Barcelona Rosselló, 87-89. Tel. 93 322 81 61

xavier güell

gaudíguide

GG100
1902-2002

Original translation: Graham Thomson
Revised translation: Trevor Foskett
Graphic Designer: Toni Cabré, Editorial Gustavo Gili, SA

© Xavier Güell, 2002

© Editorial Gustavo Gili, SA, Barcelona 2002

Printed in Spain
ISBN: 84-252-1870-5
Depósito legal: B. 9.488-2002
Printed by: Ingoprint, SA, Barcelona

Contents

Introduction

Antoni Gaudí i Cornet was born in the city of Reus (Tarragona province, Spain) on the 25th of June, 1852. He went to the Pious School in Reus, run by the Piarist Fathers, and then studied at the Barcelona Provincial School of Architecture, receiving his diploma on the 15th of March, 1878. Even before he finished studying architecture, Gaudí started collaborating in 1877 in the studio of the architect Josep Fontseré, continuing until 1882. He worked with Fontseré on designing the details for one of the most important projects then being undertaken in the city of Barcelona, the Parc de la Ciutadella. The main gates of this large park are thought to have been partly designed by Gaudí.

In 1878, in response to a public competition, he designed and manufactured two lampposts for the plaça Reial in Barcelona. His very first works, still to be seen in their original site, thus mark the beginnings of Gaudí's links with Barcelona, the city that was to be the geographical setting for almost all his later activity. Gaudí's most important works are all in Barcelona.

From 1883 until his death in 1926, Gaudí completed ten different schemes in Barcelona. These varied schemes included private houses, schools, apartment buildings in the Eixample ("Ensanche" in Spanish, the expansion of the city following a grid plan), gatehouses, an estate planned as a garden city, and even a cathedral, the Sagrada Familia.

I would like to emphasize the Sagrada Familia for several reasons. The main, and perhaps most interesting reason is that the normal way of trying to understand a contemporary architect's work is by studying their work in its chronological sequence, but in Gaudí's case, we can also study his work on a single project, the Sagrada Familia, over the course of his entire career.

Yet to really understand the changes in Gaudí's ideas for the Sagrada Familia, we have to see them in the context of the other buildings he worked on during his career. The development of Gaudí's career as an architect is clearly reflected in the order of his different projects, which should be seen as a constant effort to discover new solutions, based on his progress in the preceding project.

From 1883 to 1890, Gaudí was completing the crypt of the Sagrada Familia at the same time as working on the construction of the Vicens House, the Capricho in Comillas, the gatehouses on the Güell estate, and the Güell Palace. The eclectic nature of this period should be interpreted as his reliance on a variety of different styles.

Between 1891 and 1990, Gaudí built the cathedral's apse and began the Nativity facade, which has to be understood in the context of Gaudí's construction of the Episcopal Palace in Astorga, the Teresian Convent, the Fernández Andrés House in León and the Calvet House. This was a period with its roots in the neo-Gothic, which undoubtedly served as a point of departure, although Gaudí did not forget to «make a commitment to absolute sincerity», a phrase coined by the architect and teacher Eugène Emmanuel Viollet-le-Duc (1814-1879).

From 1901 to 1926, Gaudí was working on the cathedral's Nativity facade and, from 1903 onwards, on its bell towers. These should be understood in the context of the other works he produced in this period, his most fruitful period, the period that made him an internationally recognized architect: the Bellesguard House, Park Güell, the wall and gate for the Miralles estate, the restoration of the Cathedral in Palma de Mallorca, the Batlló House, the Milà

House, the crypt for the Colonia Güell and the Sagrada Familia schoolrooms. These years at the start of the 20th century were marked by works that were exceptional, individual, assured and daring. This willingness to take risks is particularly important, and should be seen as rather antisocial and the main reason for his feeling of being isolated and misunderstood during the last ten years of his working life, when he obstinately dedicated himself to making an impossible dream come true.

The reader of this guide can thus make a parallel reading, relating the work of the different phases of the construction of the Sagrada Familia to the other constructions Gaudí was working at the same time, though the Sagrada Familia is of course also considered as a single work in its own right.

The many commissions Gaudí received over the course of his career allow us to divide his work, in this introduction, into several features that are worth considering separately. These range from very general features, such as the urban context, to ones relating more to design and detail. To put it another way, this approach corresponds to the process starting with the first sketch designs for each project, clearly entirely Gaudí's own ideas, and finishing with the final design and its construction, with the help of his large team of collaborators.

Gaudí developed all of his schemes in basically the same way. He started with his initial ideas on how to place the building in its context, whether a clearly defined context or one lacking any sort of co-ordinates, and designed everything, down to the most minute ornamental details, whether on the main facade or hidden away in a corner of one of the inner rooms. The first examples of Gaudí's work we are going to consider are the Vicens House and the Sagrada Familia. The Vicens House is interesting because it is an example of Gaudí's very early work, showing how he approached the problem of siting the building in the irregular grid of narrow streets forming the Gràcia district of Barcelona. Gaudí sets his house against the wall to the east, enjoying the view to the south along carrer Aulèstia i Pijoan, in order to obtain two contrasting views, one from the city landscape and one from the house's garden, where he built two interesting features: a compact, cylindrical gazebo with a dome and spire on the western corner, and a free-standing structure originally intended to be a fountain, that was very similar to the arch formerly belonging to the Güell family that is still standing near the Faculty of Pharmacy. The house is sited so as to prevent direct access from the street, while stepped brickwork is used to make the metal gate, with its motif of fan palm leaves, merge with the facade of the house. This was when Gaudí was considering how to site the Sagrada Familia in its urban context, and his answer was very different, because its context was very different. The siting of the Sagrada Familia fits in perfectly with the Cerdà Plan (the grid plan for Barcelona's expansion), and is absolutely Cartesian, except for its proportions. Gaudí occupies the entire possible length of the north-south axis of the block with the building's floor plan, neglecting to leave space for the main access to the cathedral. His solution, a great flight of steps leading up to the "House of God" is still valid, but he uses the large flat area in front of the three doors to resolve the conflict between the vehicles on carrer Mallorca and pedestrian access to the cathedral. Gaudí did not come up with a pragmatic solution for something as important as the frontal view of the main facade with its essential stepped plinth. His study to ensure optimum visibility for the cathedral reveals the complex fragmentation of these sightlines.

I should add that the Latin cross layout means the cathedral's other axis (east-west) is completely within the limits of the city block. Whether the main facade ought to face south rather than west is a different question, and this is not the place to consider it.

As already mentioned, Gaudí's work can be considered in two different ways. One is to study his works from 1880 to 1926 in their chronological order, and the other way to consider his work is to focus on a single building, the Sagrada Familia, on which he worked from 1883 to 1926. It is particularly interesting to consider the parallel nature of the two, as it allows us to see the connections and contacts between the sequence of other works Gaudí built and the Sagrada Familia. The reason for this interest in the sequential nature of his work lies in the fact that there are a number of quite evident similarities, as well as several contradictions. In any case, Gaudí's remarkable work is unique because it can be considered in both a fragmentary fashion, project by project, and as a whole, through his lifetime's work on the Sagrada Familia.

The next scheme to be discussed is the Güell Palace (1886-1889), and more specifically by commenting the section along an axis cutting the body of the main hall. Gaudí sites this main hall at the geometrical centre of the palace. This resolves a whole series of questions, ranging from the treatment of the hall as a sort of central courtyard surrounded by rooms on different levels, to ensuring greater privacy, achieved by distancing the main space from the two facades, the main facade and the rear. This space forms the heart of the building and is used by people on their way from one room to another, but it is also a place of worship, as there is an altar concealed behind elaborate, lavishly decorated doors. In the hall, the light gives the effect of a church, with sunlight only entering directly through openings in the roof vault and as diffuse light through the rose windows, though it also recalls the natural light deep within a forest. At the time religious spaces were usually intended to be dark and gloomy, and this would have applied to Gaudí's huge (170 m tall) parabolic central dome for the Sagrada Familia that, while he was working on the Güell Palace, must have seemed a remote ideal.

Gaudí's building for the Teresian religious order (1888-1890) is not at all dark and gloomy. It would be out of place to interpret the stark construction of the Teresian building, whose design is controlled and austere, in terms of the design of the Sagrada Familia, which is full of variants in form and construction. If we compare the ground plans of the two buildings, we can see that, in the first, Gaudí uses a small hypostyle hall (one with a roof supported by columns) at the eastern and western ends of the floors occupied by the dormitories. These spaces, which should be understood as the "beginning and end" of the cloister, are brightly lit by light entering along the two courtyards. The feeling of an elongated cloister this creates is best appreciated on the first floor, as on the upper floors the internal courtyards are larger and the corridor linking the adjacent classrooms does not have the same beautiful proportions as the one on the first floor.

In Gaudí's project for the cathedral, the cloister's conception and location is innovative. Rather than being merely a kind of annexe, with a square ground plan, connected at a single point to the central nave of the church, it is turned into a feature running around the building's entire perimeter. This conception of the cloister as a shock absorber, absorbing the bustle of the city and insulating the interior from the outside world, is surprisingly different from the idea of the cloister as a square annexe. The idea of isolation underlying the cathedral's cloister is bold, and even rather disconcerting when considered as a reflection on the relationship between architecture and religion.

This similarity between a long closed cloister and an open perimeter cloister is a response to the site, and to the role of the cloister in bringing together the members of a community, which in one case is closed ("cloistered"), and in the other is open to the city.

Almost in strict chronological sequence, the next piece of work considered is the Calvet House (1898-1904). This coincided with an important period in the construction of the cathedral. When Gaudí started construction of the bell towers, he thought their ground plan should be square and rotated through forty-five degrees, so that the salient edge, the arris, at the junction of the two faces would lighten the excessively heavy effect of the Nativity facade. Just as he was about to start building the two pairs of free-standing towers, he decided the geometry had to be changed, and adopted a new, circular, ground plan. Obviously, when two circles are drawn within two squares the corners of the squares remain exposed. Gaudí resolved this by incorporating a feature that can be interpreted as belvederes or balconies. Note that the texture of the stonework on the Calvet House and on the bell towers is almost the same.

On the facade of the Calvet House, and in contrast to what other architects of the time were doing on houses with a similar programme, Gaudí has placed a single, enclosed, angled bay window precisely on the entrance axis, but only on the main floor. The rest of the facade houses the openings, all of the same size, of the bedroom windows on the different floors, which are protected with metal railings, all of the same size. This is very unusual for residential buildings in the Eixample, and emphasizes the single feature projecting from the facade, the bay window. We can compare the balconies of the Sagrada Familia, created by the interplay of geometrical shapes, and the single bay window, both of which are really quite small.

In 1906, Gaudí was commissioned to build the Milà House (the Milà i Camps family house), which is commonly known as *La Pedrera* (the quarry). The site has three facades and was large enough for the building to be approached as two independent units. This prompted the creation of two courtyards, one completely circular, on the chamfered corner of carrer Provença and the Passeig de Gràcia, and a second courtyard, also with circular ends, but elongated parallel to carrer Provença. Returning to the Sagrada Familia, comparing the ground plan of one of the bell towers to that of this circular courtyard, we can see there are clear similarities. The plan of the bell tower consists of two concentric rings and an internal staircase, adapting to the limits of the facade and the adjacent walls. This undoubtedly structural concept profoundly influenced the construction of *La Pedrera*.

If we recall the tambour with twelve cylindrical columns used to resolve the previously mentioned change in geometry in the plan of the bell towers, we can see it as being the true support for the bell towers. Standing inside the bell towers and looking upwards, and then doing the same in the circular courtyard of the Milà House, we can see just how similar these two inner faces are, both of them almost sheer.

Now look at how the exterior of the bell towers has been handled, and compare it with the facade of *La Pedrera*. Note the slanting block of stone that directs the sound of the bells down to the neighbourhood below, and note its strong resemblance to the profile and section of the facade of *La Pedrera*. There is a clear similarity between this slanting piece of stone and the little windows located on the terrace roof.

Looking hard, further similarities can be found. Consider a fragment of one of the bell towers, open it up longitudinally, and flatten it out to produce a flat surface. Superimposing this onto the facade of *La Pedrera* we see that both have the same number of openings and, likewise, the same number of circular columns (twelve) supporting the facade. Of course, this process has to be applied to each of the courtyards, and putting the two together forms the plane that, like a huge sheet or blanket, forms the three faces of the facade. We might add a further detail: the Milà House's entire facade, with its three faces (in accordance with the Cerdà plan), is built in a single material, subtly assisted by Josep Maria Jujol's wrought iron railings. Gaudí completed this house in 1910, while the bell towers of the Sagrada Familia were slowly being built. *La Pedrera* was the last completely new work that Gaudí was to carry through to completion.

Construction did not begin on the chapel commissioned by Eusebi Güell for his new textile factory in Santa Coloma de Cervelló until 1908, after ten years of tests and trials.

In this project we can see how Gaudí, once more, made full use of the opportunity to further his studies of construction and structures. His experience during the construction of the Sagrada Familia had shown some things had to be changed. Gaudí was evidently dissatisfied with the final shape of the crypt of the cathedral, even after he had made a number of slight changes to Villar y Lozano's design. As a result, he took a significant step forward in the structural design of this new chapel in the textile colony, reducing thrust, and again using abstract shapes in order to develop his ideas for the space. Gaudí's intentions for the appearance of the chapel as a whole are only known from a couple of his sketches. They show a combination of features similar to Milà House, though they also recall the Sagrada Familia.

I would like to conclude this introduction by drawing the reader's attention to two interior spaces. The first is the roof space of the Milà House where, before it was adapted for use as attic apartments, it was possible to appreciate the construction based on of a series of parabolic arches with the handmade bricks laid in only two stretcher-bonded courses; the second is the interior space of the crypt. In both, light enters from the side; in both, the arches are held together by the continuous thread of the key course; in both, the same precedent is apparent, the attic floor of the Bellesguard House.

Works built in Barcelona

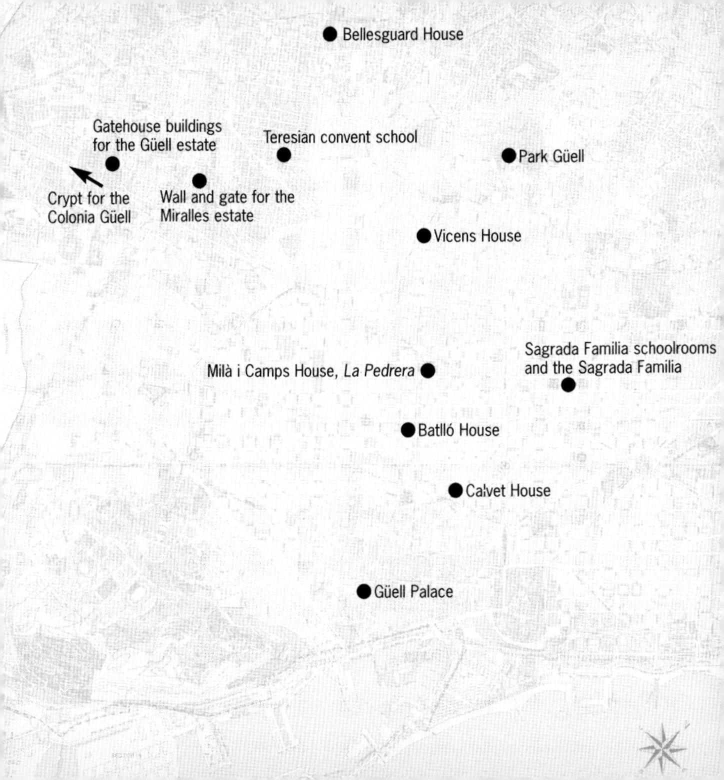

● Bellesguard House

Gatehouse buildings
for the Güell estate
● Teresian convent school
● Park Güell

Crypt for the
Colonia Güell
Wall and gate for the
Miralles estate

● Vicens House

Milà i Camps House, *La Pedrera* ●

Sagrada Familia schoolrooms
and the Sagrada Familia
●

● Batlló House

● Calvet House

● Güell Palace

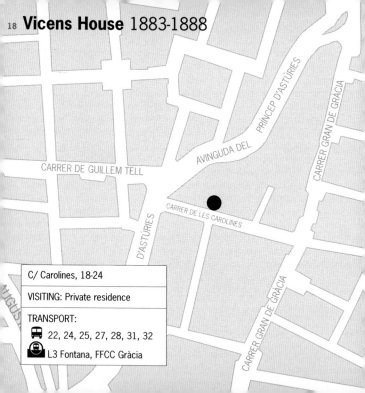

Vicens House 1883-1888

CARRER DE GUILLEM TELL

AVINGUDA DEL

PRINCEP D'ASTÚRIES

CARRER GRAN DE GRÀCIA

CARRER DE LES CAROLINES

D'ASTÚRIES

AUGUST

CARRER GRAN DE GRÀCIA

C/ Carolines, 18-24

VISITING: Private residence

TRANSPORT:

22, 24, 25, 27, 28, 31, 32

L3 Fontana, FFCC Gràcia

This summer residence for the tile manufacturer Manuel Vicens Montaner was the first work Gaudí built as an architect.

Clearly oriental in inspiration, it is rooted in Arabic and Mudejar architecture. The way the design uses decorated tiles is remarkable, as only two models of tile are used on the facades to clad this unusual building, which is strikingly unusual in the context of the Gràcia district of Barcelona. This tile cladding wraps the two main storeys of the building - the ground and first floor - in horizontal bands, while on the attic and roof floors the tiling forms vertical lines that split when they reach the roof floor. The interaction and compensation of the vertical lines and the horizontal bands clearly juxtaposes them, giving the house a compact look. Another interesting feature is the metal railing separating it from the street. The house then had a large garden running to the main road (avinguda Princep d'Asturies), containing several features such as a large fountain, flower beds and a pavilion in one corner, and so the house could be seen from a distance sufficient to give perspective.

A section of the railing (fan palm leaves) that used to run around the garden now forms part of the main entrance to Park Güell, on carrer Olot.

The architect Serra Martínez, almost doubling its original volume but following the same criteria and preserving the unity of style, extended the house in 1925. This is a private residence, and so one cannot visit the internal spaces (drawing rooms, dining room, smoking room and so on), which can only be studied by consulting photographs.

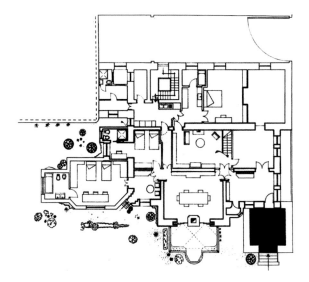

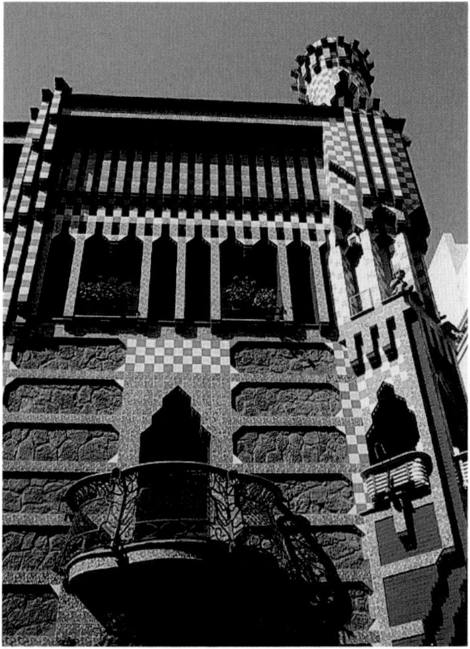

Elevation of the facade on carrer Carolines, drawing by Enric Serra Grau.
Elevation of the facade overlooking the garden, drawing by Fco. Javier Saura Manich.

View of the house from the former garden. The garden is now occupied by a block of flats on the corner with avinguda Príncep d'Astúries.

Gatehouse buildings for the Güell estate 1884-1887

JARDINS DEL PALAU
DE PEDRALBES

CARRER DE FERNANDO PRIMO DE RIVERA

AVINGUDA DE PEDRALBES

DIAGONAL

PLAÇA DE
PIUS XII

Avinguda de Pedralbes, 7

VISITING: Now occupied by the Catedra
Gaudí, (Chair of Gaudí Studes), open to
the public during termtime.

TRANSPORT:

63, 78

L3 Palau Reial

This small construction should be understood as two buildings on either side of a large gate, thus controlling access to a large recreational estate belonging to the Güell family.

If we study the layout of the two buildings, clearly designed to effectively control access to the estate, we can see the change from solid walls to an almost open sloping plane that provides an unrestricted view of the garden area around the two buildings. The smaller building was the gatekeeper's lodge, and the larger one was a coach-house and stables. The gatekeeper's lodge, which stands to the left of the large gate, consists of one space with an octagonal plan, covered by a cupola and topped by a spire, and two other rectangular spaces, all of them in the same style. The stables, to the right of the gate, are immediately adjacent to the turret supporting the great iron gate with its figure of a dragon. This dragon, intended to intimidate intruders, introduces dynamic tension to the relationship between the two buildings, and uses wrought iron in several different ways. The whole composed by this iron gate and the gate for pedestrians (to its left) quite clearly indicates the tremendous effort that Gaudí consistently put into designing the "auxiliary" elements in most of his schemes. The stable building, which currently houses the Chair of Gaudí Studies, consists of two sections. The first section has a small hallway, while the second section is larger and rectangular and uses parabolic arches and a parabolic roof as the architectural features supporting and covering the space within.

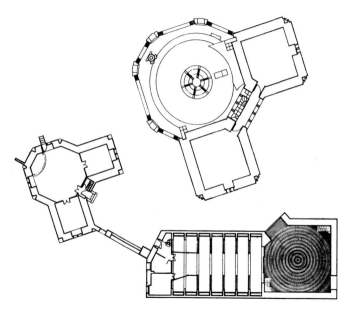

Perspective drawing of the stable block.

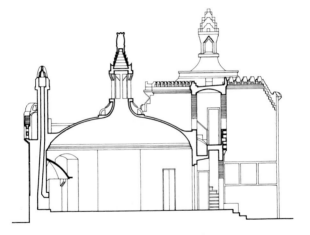

Section of the porter's lodge.

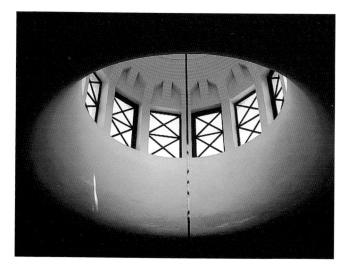

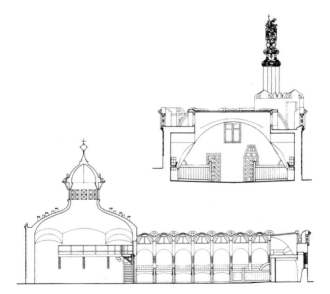

Sections of the stables.

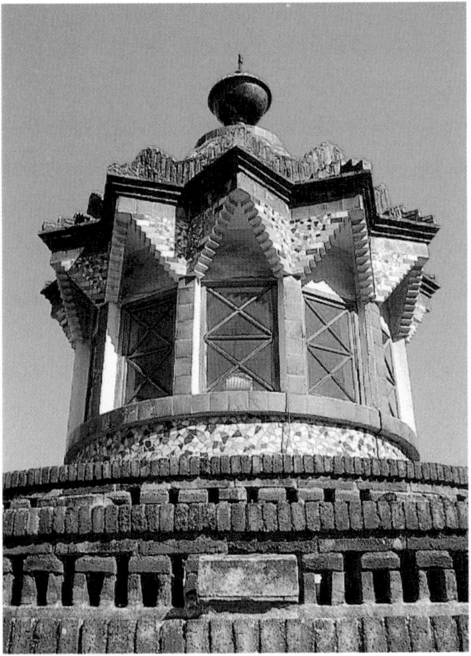

View of the space now occupied by the Department of Gaudí Studies.

Güell Palace 1886-1889

CARRER DE LA UNIÓ

MARQUÈS DE BARBERÀ

LA RAMBLA

PLAÇA
REIAL

C. COLOM

CARRER NOU DE LA RAMBLA

PL. DEL
TEATRE

RAMBLA

C/ Nou de la Rambla, 9

VISITING: Tuesday to Saturday 11.00 to
14.00 and from 16.00 to 19.00. Special
visits by arrangement with the Servei
de Patrimoni Arquitectònic (Diputació
de Barcelona), tel. 93 402 21 73.

TRANSPORT:

🚌 14, 38, 59, 91

 L3 Liceu

The construction of this new Barcelona residence for Eusebi Güell i Bacigalupi, industrialist, intellectual, great patron of the arts in general and of Gaudí in particular, coincided with one of the most splendid moments in the city's history, the preparations for the Universal Exposition of 1888.

Alongside its specific function as a family house, the new residence was intended to host some of the grandest social events of its day, as well as cultural evenings and discussions. Gaudí drew many studies for the main facade, and presented just two of them for Güell to choose from, with his client deciding on the project that Gaudí himself preferred. The palace, now the property of Barcelona Provincial Council, should be visited with some care, since each floor is of quite exceptional interest.

The basement floor, with its great cylindrical pillars of handmade brick that finish in wide truncated cone capitals, was occupied by the stables, with access by way of a spiral ramp leading down from ground level. On the ground floor, the two arches (a separate entrance and exit) unmistakably forming the main access to the palace were designed to accommodate the carriages of the time. They lead the visitor to the flight of stairs, located between them, which then passes through a mezzanine and proceeds up to the main floor of the building. This is exclusively given over to several drawing rooms and salons for holding receptions. The large main hall is absolutely unique, and is the heart of the building. Its ceiling is a cupola, recalling the dome at the crossing of the transept and the nave of a church. This elaborate and complex cupola includes some small circular openings that dimly illuminate the space.

The upper floor, following a conventional layout, is occupied by bedrooms.

Elevation of the main facade, drawing by Rosa Cortés Pagés.

However, just before entering this area, there is a mezzanine where Güell had his office, with a balcony overlooking the central hall.

The top floor was the servants' quarters. It is not particularly interesting, in keeping with the limited value usually given to this kind of space.

The lower floors of the main facade are clad in marble, creating the effect of a plinth, making the finish more palatial and urbane. Above this the cladding is masonry, giving a rather old-fashioned look, which is also used on the rear facade, at the same levels. The entrance, which we mentioned above, is perfectly symmetrical, and is indicated by the openings of the two parabolic archways. The positioning of these openings, the large gallery running almost the entire length of the facade, the parapet with its discreet little stepped crenellations complementing the chimneys, and the ventilation shafts, no two the same, all come together to compose this perfectly rhythmic plane, greyish-white in colour and recalling Venetian Gothic.

The south-facing rear facade has an unusual feature, projecting from the stone plane of the facade: a gallery with rounded ends under a balcony and pergola. This composite feature is like a large blind, coming down to shelter the back of the house from the hot summer sun.

The interior of the palace has been treated with an exceptional wealth of detail. Wooden panelling, marble columns, stucco work, delicate wrought iron items, marquetry work and specially designed furniture give every room of the house a quality of its own, quite different from the rest.

Cross-section.

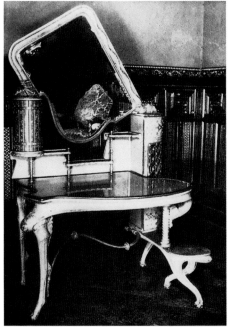

These items of furniture from the Güell Palace, a dressing table and two chairs, are in the Gaudí House Museum in Park Güell. (See page 140)

Folding screen and chair from the dining room. Private collection.

Teresian convent school 1888-1890

CARRER DE CALATRAVA

CARRER D'ALACANT

CARRER DE GANDUXER

CARRER DE JOSEP

CARRER DE TORRAS

CARRER SANT CASIMIR

GENERAL MITRE

CARRER FREIXA

C/ Ganduxer, 85-105

VISITING: Saturdays from 10.00 to 12.00.
Permission to view the interior can be
requested from the nun at the door.

TRANSPORT:

🚌 14, 16, 70, 72, 74

 FFCC Les Tres Torres

Right from the beginning, this free-standing building, rectangular in plan (approximately 58 x 18 metres) was designed to be a school. Overall, at first glance, it might be taken for an industrial building, because of the materials used and the repetitive nature of the four facades.

Certain aspects of this building should be noted. Look at the main facade, and note how the height of the windows, each within a perfectly fashioned parabolic arch, varies according to whether they are on the ground, first, second or third floor. Just as in the residential buildings of the Eixample district, the difference in height of the window openings shows the lower floors were considered more important than the upper floors.

Gaudí resolved the functional requirements by locating the classrooms and related rooms on the ground and first floors, while the second and third floors are taken up by dormitories for the boarding pupils.

The corridors on the ground and first floors are another interesting feature of the internal spaces. A perfectly centred corridor runs from one end of the building to the other, giving access to the rooms. On the floor above, this space is divided. The single corridor unfolds, opening out to form courtyards that provide light for the new route. Circulation along the different corridors is in different directions, recalling the monastery cloisters of medieval architecture. The corridors again use parabolic arches, seeking to create a more secluded space that is more suitable for contemplation and prayer.

Returning to the facades, note the four turrets, one on each of the four corners. Crowning each is a characteristic feature of Gaudí's architecture, a four-armed ceramic cross, with two horizontals at right angles.

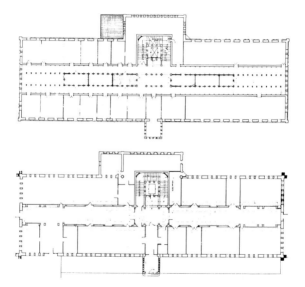

General ground floor plans, drawing by Lluís Bonet.

The building, built with limited money, is austere and rational, unlike most of Gaudí's work, but this fully meets its requirements and is a perfect response to the content within.

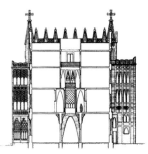

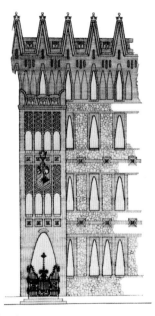

Detail of the main facade.

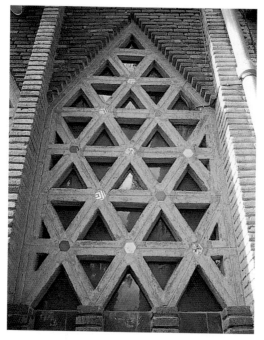

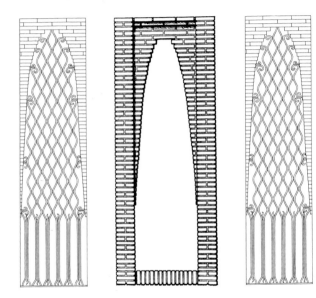

The masonry walls have large windows framed by bricks,
drawing by Joan Bergós Massó. The grilles covering the windows.

Images of two classrooms at the time when the school was inaugurated.

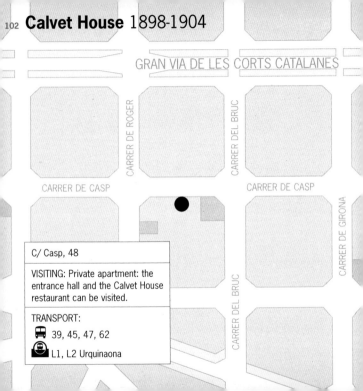

GRAN VIA DE LES CORTS CATALANES

CARRER DE ROGER

CARRER DEL BRUC

CARRER DE CASP

CARRER DE CASP

CARRER DE GIRONA

CARRER DEL BRUC

C/ Casp, 48

VISITING: Private apartment: the
entrance hall and the Calvet House
restaurant can be visited.

TRANSPORT:

39, 45, 47, 62

L1, L2 Urquinaona

This is the first of Gaudí's blocks of flats in the Eixample. It is on a gap site, and was built for the family of the textile manufacturer Pedro Calvet.

Although outwardly very similar in appearance to other buildings in this part of the Eixample, entering the building's entrance hall reveals a whole series of striking details. The doorknocker on the main street door, the bell plaque, the number 48, all emphasise the city feel of the ground floor; Gaudí produced wonderful designs for all the furniture in the offices. If we enter the hallway, we see it is divided into compartments. After passing through the first compartment, the visitor is welcomed to the second by benches with elliptical mirrors set against the wall. A little further on, there are some columns with surprisingly complex ornamentation, forerunners of the columns supporting the enclosed balcony in the Batlló House. Other more baroque columns surround the lift-cage, which recalls a baldachin (a canopy-like structure over an altar), but with a hole in its centre so the lift can reach the other floors of the building. Walking up the stairs to the first floor we can look closely at the finish of the doors of the different apartments, whose peepholes and other pieces of metalwork deserve to be considered as pieces of jewellery.

As mentioned above, the main facade is of limited interest, in sharp contrast to the rear facade, which overlooks the courtyard in the interior of the block. As there is no public access, it can only be studied in photographs, in common with a number of Gaudí's other buildings. This is one of the few houses in Barcelona's Eixample where, thanks to Gaudí's commitment to his work, we have a facade with bay windows coming off the living rooms, treated in similar fashion to the rear facade of the Güell Palace, together with balconies

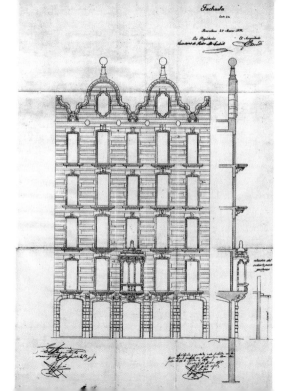

with beautifully designed railings. It is worth pointing out how unusual this is, since the approach generally adopted in the design of the rear facades of residential buildings in the Eixample is to use a continuous roofed gallery, with relatively elaborate carpentry detailing, the aim being to provide abundant light, and to make best use of the sun's light and warmth. The restaurant located on the ground floor retains some original elements from Pedro Calvet's office, and its atmosphere has been preserved by a careful restoration.

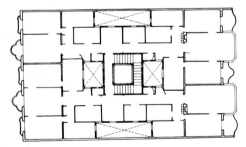

General floor plan.

Cross-section of the lobby, drawing by Ma. Isabel Herrero Campos.

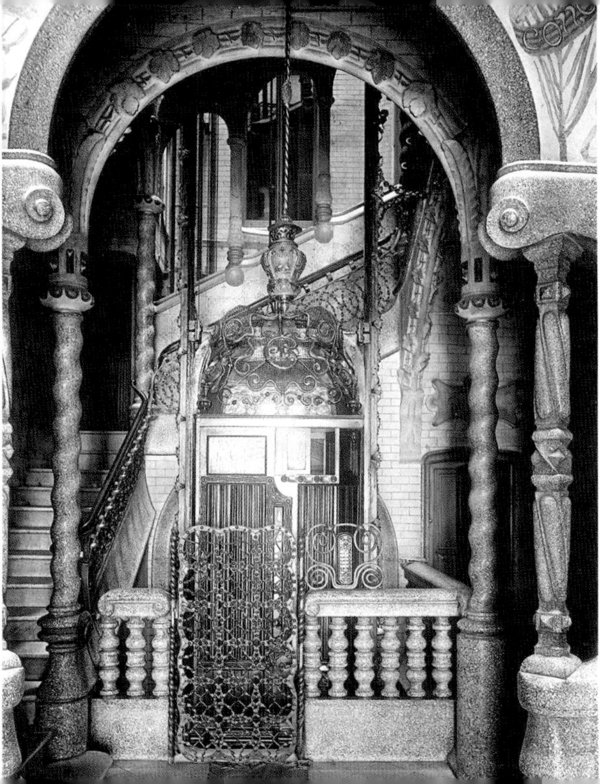

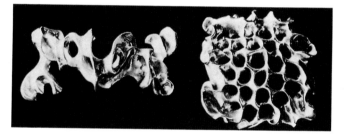

Detail showing the door handle and the covering for the peephole in the door.

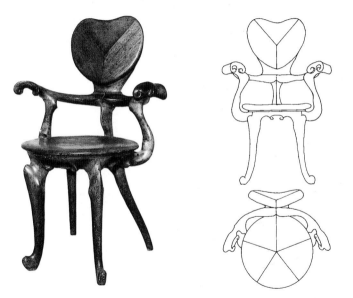

Chair with arms from the commercial office in Calvet House.

Chairs and sofa from the commercial office in Calvet House.

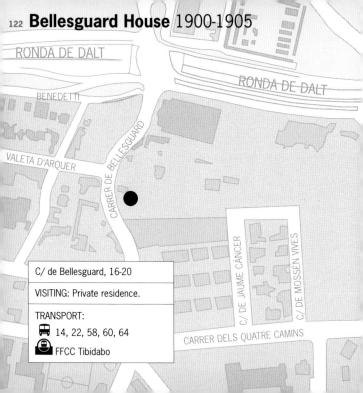

RONDA DE DALT

RONDA DE DALT

BENEDETTI

VALETA D'ARQUER

CARRER DE BELLESGUARD

CARRER DE JAUME CÀNCER

CARRER DE MOSSÈN VIVES

CARRER DELS QUATRE CAMINS

C/ de Bellesguard, 16-20

VISITING: Private residence.

TRANSPORT:

14, 22, 58, 60, 64

FFCC Tibidabo

The house was built at the base of the Collserola range of hills, in the area where Martí l'Humà (King Martin the Humane), the last of the Catalan dynasty, had built his residence. This is the project Gaudí was working on at the turn of the century. The design is greatly influenced by respect for the past, with the house rising up as a solid block, opaque and enclosed within itself, that Gaudí seeks to make clear is defensive.

This idea of an isolated site to be defended continues with the tall narrow geminate and triform window openings, except in the area above the main entrance, where balconies breaks this sheer, hard plane.

Only if one is lucky enough to see the inside of the house, unlikely as it is a private residence, can one see how this harsh defensive style is transformed into something much more gentle, creating a peaceful, pleasant and understanding atmosphere in a white setting. The upper part of the stairwell, just where it arrives at the attic level, is lit by a window which, with a geometrical composition and evident Arabic influences, bathes this upper area in coloured light, thus reducing the intensity of light.

The attic under the roof, executed using brickwork arches with lightened facings, is a further example of Gaudí's skilled use of brickwork, and shows how his design and construction skills had developed. Gaudí again gives great importance to the corners of the building, crowning them with towers, one clearly intended to support one of his typical four-armed crosses, as if held aloft by a valiant warrior.

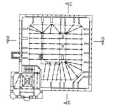

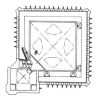

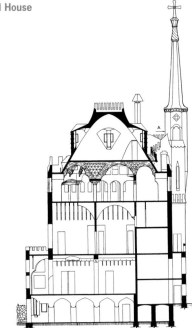

Cross section.

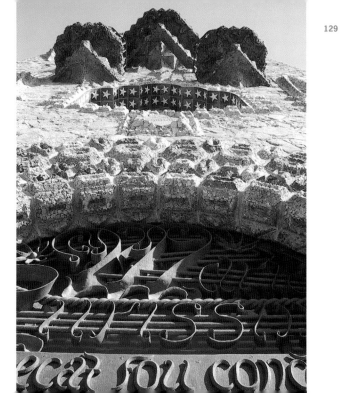

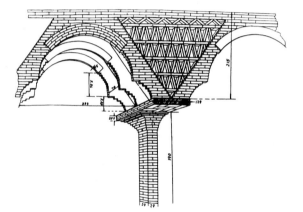

Structure of the roofing, showing the traditional brickwork construction, drawing by Joan Bergós Massó.

PARK GÜELL

C/ Olot, s/n

COLLABORATING ARCHITECTS:
Josep Maria Jujol and Joan Rubió i Bellver

VISITING: City park open to the
public during the hours of daylight.

TRANSPORT:
24, 25, 87
L3 Lesseps, Vallcarca

TRAVESSERA DE DALT

This is the largest work, in terms of its area, that Gaudí undertook in Barcelona. The intention for the 20-hectare site was to lay it out, provide the services and, ultimately, to create a garden city comparable to the ones that appeared in England in the late 19th century. This is why the English "Park" was used in preference to the Catalan "Parc".

Park Güell is the most important piece of work that Gaudí finished in his entire career as an architect, in that it is the most complete. In its execution, he relied on the collaboration of the architect Josep Maria Jujol for all the elements involving colour. Take a careful look at the architecture of the two gatehouse buildings on either side of the main entrance on carrer Olot: the buildings are quite unique in their own right, yet they are comparable to the gatehouse buildings for the Güell estate on the avinguda de Pedralbes, as both are intended to control access to a private estate.

A great deal of the work in Park Güell is related to infrastructure for the estate, including some stunning features, such as the hypostyle hall (the hall of columns), and the large plaza it supports with a long sinusoidal bench around its perimeter. Finally, note how the project is designed to fit into the topography of the site, using features like viaducts, elevated walkways and certain individual elements, recalling palm trees, that act as references to their environment.

Gaudí's approach to the urban design of the Park is also interesting, as he considered the residential area as somewhere enclosed, a space to be defended. A few years after its completion the site was acquired by the city authorities as part of its architectural heritage, and in 1984 it was declared a World Heritage Site by UNESCO.

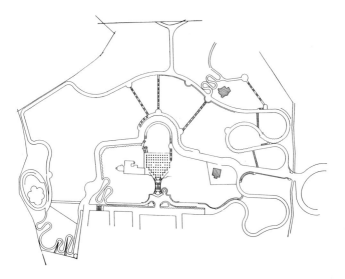

General plan of Park Güell, drawing by César Martinell.

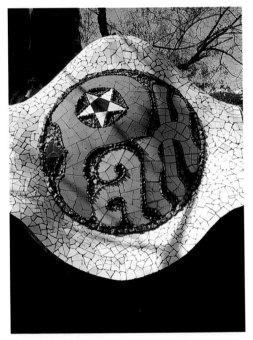

After these initial points, some more general comments on Park Güell. The gatehouse buildings at the main entrance, one designed as the gatekeeper's residence and the other (on the left) as a waiting room and meeting point for visitors, are quite unique. By placing these two buildings on either side of the gap in the stone wall, Gaudí wanted them to be seen as castle keeps, jealously protecting the enclosure and the residential development within. This rather Medieval feeling (inward-looking and secretive) is brought perfectly up to date by the use of colour, precisely at the point where he presents us with this image of the impregnable tower. The cambered surfaces of the roofs are covered with *trencadís* ceramic fragments and topped by the mushroom Gaudí frequently used as a decorative motif, the fly agaric (*Amanita muscaria*). The geometric composition created by the surfaces of these roofs is, on its own, sufficient to class Gaudí as an architect of genius.

Passing between the gatehouses brings us to an area leading to a flight of steps, with a fountain and the figure of a salamander, all of them clad in *trencadís* and combining together to create a delightful effect. The steps lead us to the great hypostyle hall with its 86 columns, planned by Gaudí to be the ideal site for the market stalls selling fresh produce for the residents. Note the four "medallions" and adjoining motifs set in the ceiling, like keystones, and taking the place of four of the columns.

Continuing up the steps, we reach the great platform with its commanding view of the coastal plain occupied by Barcelona. We should pay particular attention here to the winding, serpentine, edge of the platform, which takes the form of a bench that shimmers in the strong sunlight, giving the impression of movement. Gaudí consistently used animals and plants as a point of

reference in his architecture, and we should perhaps interpret this bench as a snake, with rather unusually coloured markings, basking in the full sun and enjoying the warmth and intense sunshine of the Mediterranean sun.

The ceramic cladding (*trencadís*, literally "jigsaw-puzzle") based on broken pieces of decorative tile, old broken tiles, and even in some places, bits of old plates, china dolls and glass wine jars, turns this bench, intended for relaxation, conversation and rest, into a huge and unprecedented collage.

Finally, we must mention the features forming the infrastructure required to reach all the different parts of the park: viaducts, retaining walls, elevated walkways and several one-off features.

The viaducts are a good example of Gaudí's dialogue with the site's steep and rugged relief. Some are decorated, while others are simple cylindrical columns that perfectly meet the structural demands. They are all built in stone from the site, roughly finished, but perfectly positioned. In the places intended to be covered in ivy, the stones are small; where the wall has to be strong, it is inclined, forming a chiaroscuro with classical roots, and the stony mass is rougher. Where there are steep bends the columns are modelled on helicoid spirals, suggesting change and movement. Where the route is less steep, there are some planters rather like palm trees, with the shaft and capital recalling the stem and the tuft of leaves.

Where the way takes on a more agile movement, becoming an elevated walk or bridge, it is accompanied and sheltered by raised planters, while the continuous sheet of the paving is a constant point of reference.

Details of the ceiling of the hall of columns.

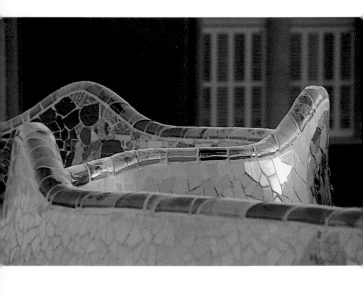

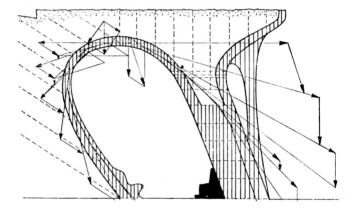

Section of a portico.

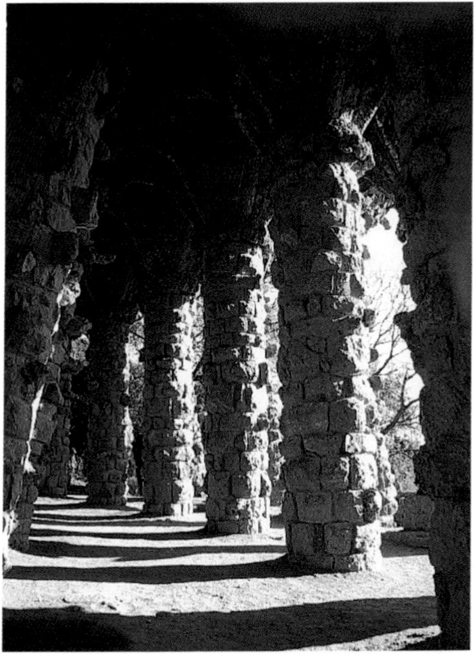

Wall and gate for the Miralles estate 1901-1902

CARRER DE FRANCESC CARBONELL

C/ DE BENET MATEU

CARRER DE MANUEL GIRONA

CARRER DEL CAPITA ARENAS

GRAN VIA DE CARLES III

C/ Manuel Girona, 55-61

TRANSPORT:

🚌 6, 16, 34, 70, 72, 74

🚇 L3 Maria Cristina

Wall and gate for the Miralles estate

This stretch of wall shows some resemblance, when seen in profile, to the wall of Park Güell, though it is simpler. Gaudí introduces a wide central opening for horse-drawn vehicles, and a second, smaller opening with a metal door for pedestrians.

The strain of the upper part of the roof covering the ensemble, of fine cement tiles manufactured by the owner of the estate, is borne by twisted metalwork converging on the four-armed cross so characteristic of Gaudí.

The bronze statue of a man on the left of the main gate, by Quim Camps, is an accurate representation of the architect Antoni Gaudí.

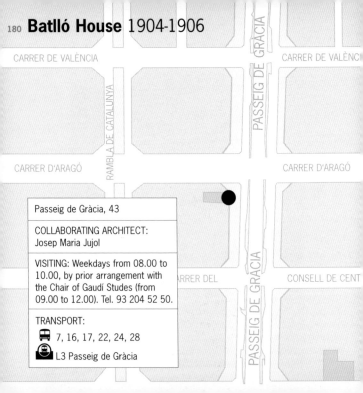

Batlló House 1904-1906

CARRER DE VALÈNCIA

CARRER DE VALÈNC

RAMBLA DE CATALUNYA

PASSEIG DE GRÀCIA

CARRER D'ARAGÓ

CARRER D'ARAGÓ

Passeig de Gràcia, 43

COLLABORATING ARCHITECT:
Josep Maria Jujol

VISITING: Weekdays from 08.00 to
10.00, by prior arrangement with
the Chair of Gaudí Studes (from
09.00 to 12.00). Tel. 93 204 52 50.

TRANSPORT:
7, 16, 17, 22, 24, 28
L3 Passeig de Gràcia

CARRER DEL

CONSELL DE CENT

PASSEIG DE GRÀCIA

This house, and the Calvet House in carrer Casp, are the only examples in the Barcelona Eixample of family houses on gap sites with a single facade, about 15 metres wide in both cases.

Before looking at the scheme, two important facts should be made clear. The first concerns the Ametller House, to the left, with its grand stepped parapet reminiscent of Flemish architecture; this was completed by the architect Josep Puig i Cadafalch in 1900, six years before Batlló House was completed. The second, a little more complex, is that Batlló House is a conversion of an existing building. In other words, when planning his design for this house, Gaudí had to transform and extend a pre-existing building. This transformation and change makes it one of the most interesting projects in Gaudí's career as an architect. What he did was to add two floors to the existing house, change the external surface ("skin") of the front and rear facades, and adapt the main floor for use as a family home by the family of José Batlló Casanovas.

Gaudí's approach to increasing the height of the main facade was to make it more slender by adding a floor and the carapace-like cornice, which recalls the shell of an animal. The two faces of the cornice are sewn together by a seam of pieces made of glazed ceramic and recalling the elbow of a medieval suit of armour. The cylindrical turret topped by the four-armed cross provides the counterpoint balancing and regulating the meeting of the silhouettes of the two houses.

The change in the building's skin is best understood by comparing it to the other facades in this part of the Eixample. Gaudí was helped by Josep Maria Jujol, a young architect who later collaborated on several of Gaudí's other

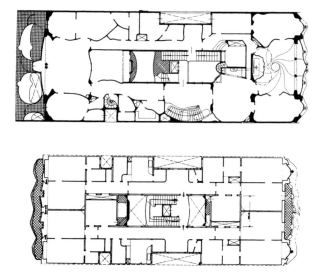

Ground plan of main floor and type floor plan, drawings by Lluís Bonet.

projects. Gaudí changed the skin on the front facade and introduced an enclosed gallery on the main floor with bone-like, skeletal, features that are clearly intended to contrast with the neighbouring house. The new skin, which is not flat but undulating, is a beautiful example of a decorated facade, recalling a medieval illuminated manuscript.

The changes in the rear facade, visible from a passageway near the corner with carrer Aragó, are simpler, since here Gaudí's design consisted of sinuous continuous balconies with fretwork balustrades running along them.

The adaptation of the main floor includes exemplary designs for all the household features: the access stairs, entirely of wood; the internal doors, some opaque and some with incorporated glass panes, which act as convex partitions to form a moveable partition "wall", whose profiles continually avoid the rectilinear; the ceilings, such as the one in the main drawing room, whose centrifugal form seeks to focus attention on the light fixture; the wooden floors, the fireplaces, as well as a new suite of furniture for the dining room, and much more. All in all, a complete set of perfectly thought-out solutions for a unique setting.

Finally, it is worth mentioning the space corresponding to the two lightwells (which are also ventilation shafts) rising from the vestibule on the ground floor and covered by a large skylight to protect them from the rain. Their walls are clad in blue and white tiles, and other stud-like ceramic elements ranging from dark to light blue, so the lightwells provide as much natural light as possible to the lower part of the building.

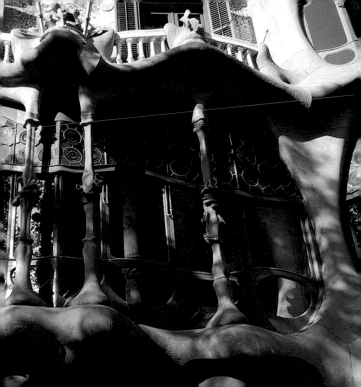

 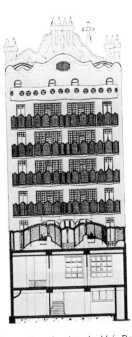

Facade seen from Passeig de Gràcia and rear view, drawings by Lluís Bonet.

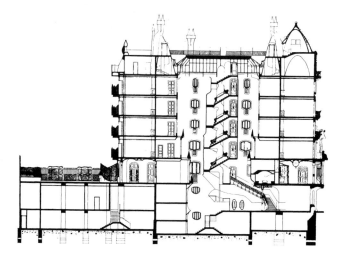

Longitudinal section.

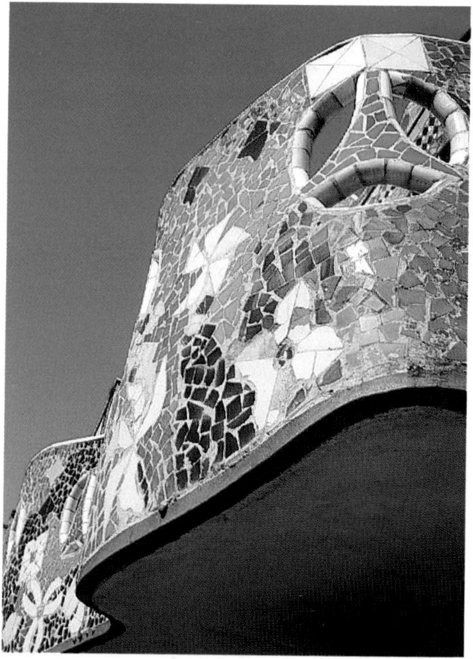

Dining room on the main floor with the furniture designed by Gaudí.

Chair matching the table in the dining room on the main floor.

Two-person chair originally belonging to the dining room on the first floor.

Milà i Camps House, *La Pedrera* 1906-1910

DIAGONAL

Passeig de Gràcia, 92, C/ Provença, 261-265

COLLABORATING ARCHITECTS:
Domènec Sugranyes, Josep Canaleta and Josep Maria Jujol

"Espai Gaudí" (the "Gaudí Space") is located in the attic and roof floors. The design for these two plants was by the architects Francisco Javier Asarta and Robert Brufau (1991-1996), and it is managed by the art historian Raquel Lacuesta. "El Pis de la Pedrera" (the "Flat in the Pedrera") is on the fourth floor. Project design and management are by Daniel Giralt-Miracle and Miguel Milà (1998-1999).

VISITING: every day 10.00-20.00.
Mondays and Fridays: a commented visit at 18.00. Open on holidays 10.00-15.00

TRANSPORT:
 7, 16, 17, 22, 24, 28, N4
L3, L5 Diagonal

CARRER DEL ROSSELLÓ

PASSEIG DE GRÀCIA

CARRER DE PROVENÇA

PAU CLARIS

CARRER DE MALLORCA

Chronologically, this was the third and last residential building Gaudí built in Barcelona's Eixample, and the only one to occupy a corner site, a chamfered corner to be precise. The house can thus be considered to have three facades: one on each street, and the third on the chamfered corner, at 45° to the other two.

Gaudí resolved this large facade by treating it as single and continuous. Looking at the other houses on the Passeig de Gràcia, we can see that most seek to emphasize how the vertical plane changes on the corner, by contrasting the different facades looking onto Passeig de Gràcia, the chamfered corner and the side street. The only breaks in the continuity of the facade are the building's two entrances, one on carrer Provença and the other on the corner itself. Providing these two entrances means the building has to be understood as follows; each entrance consists of a smaller doorway for pedestrians and a larger door for carriages. This seemingly irrelevant fact has very significant consequences.

Considering this point in more detail, the fact that the vehicle and pedestrian accesses lead straight into the two courtyards means the courtyards acquire the importance of a second facade. However this facade differs from the external facade, dominated by an effect recalling horizontal waves, because the interior facades are dominated by an almost regular vertical structure. Unusually for a house in the Eixample, the floors are all the same height, except for the taller main floor. Remaining in the two large polychrome vestibules, note that the grand flight of stairs, comparable to the one in the Batlló House, only leads to the main floor, and that there is no general staircase leading to the different apartments in a more regular, orderly

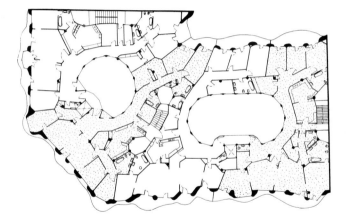

General floor plan, drawing by César Martinell.

fashion. Access is by two spacious lifts, sited next to the two main entrances, while the general staircase is relegated to a much less important role, as the service stairs.

Another point worth observing is the facade and the slightly recessed white crest crowning it on the attic level, forming the perfect support for the "spinning tops" greeting us on arriving at this belvedere floor, whose odd forms bear a startling resemblance to the figures of warriors. As in the Batlló House, Gaudí designed the protective elements such as grilles, doors and balustrades, and with Jujol's collaboration he resolved all these features perfectly. The balustrades on the balconies are excellent examples of this, not only for their lightness in contrast to the massive stone facade but also for their dramatic potential; they are based on sheet metal twisted in a really extraordinary way.

It is also possible to visit the attic floor, where each of the elements of the roof can be studied. The "Espai Gaudí" on the attic floor, has beautiful models of several of Gaudí's works.

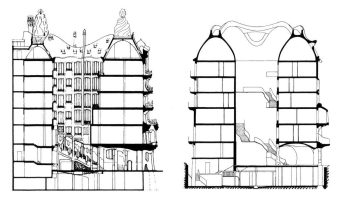

Cross-section through the circular patio and cross-section through the patio on carrer Provença, drawings by Gaudí-Groep de Delft.

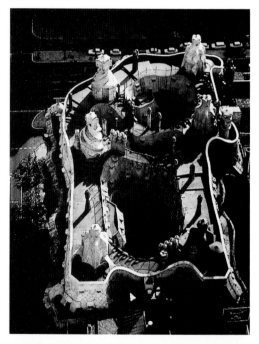

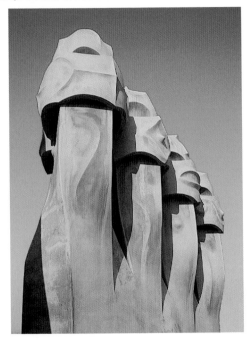

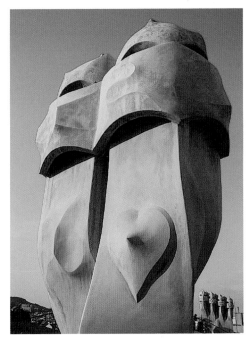

224 Milà i Camps House, *La Pedrera*

Furniture belonging to the main floor. Private collection.

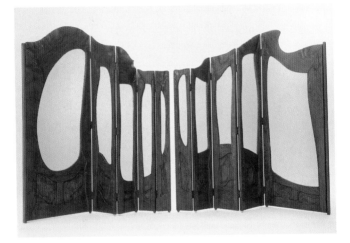

Folding screen from the main floor. Private collection.

Two wooden parquetry designs from one of the flats.

Mosaic of hydraulic paving stones.

CARRER DE LA MARINA

AVINGUDA DE GAUDÍ

CARRER DE PROVENÇA

CARRER DE SARDENYA

CARRER DE SICÍLIA

PLAÇA DE LA SAGRADA FAMÍLIA

PLAÇA DE GAUDÍ

CARRER DE MALLORCA

CARRER DE LA MARINA

CARRER DE VALÈNCIA

C/ Marina, 253 – Plaça Gaudí

VISITING: open to public from summer 2002

TRANSPORT:
19, 33, 34, 43, 44, 50, 51, 101
L2, L5 Sagrada Família

This small building on the same city block as the Sagrada Familia was intended to be provisional, and had to be built quickly and cheaply. It covers 200 m², 10 x 20 m, and can be subdivided into several different classrooms. Gaudí again uses a sine curve, but here as the structure "wrapping" the building, forming the wall and roof.

The structure, of great simplicity, is resolved by pillars supporting a long profile running down the centre of the building that supports the framework of the roof. The roof rests on the rising and falling line of the wall, and thus adopts the form of an undulating plane.

The whole structure is built in the same style of solid handmade brick. The door and window openings require lateral rabbeting, as the wall is very thin. This modest building's fragility, the fact the interior space can be divided to suit the needs of the moment, and the exemplary skill with which its form and volume have been handled all make this a lesser work of particular interest.

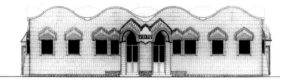

Main elevation.

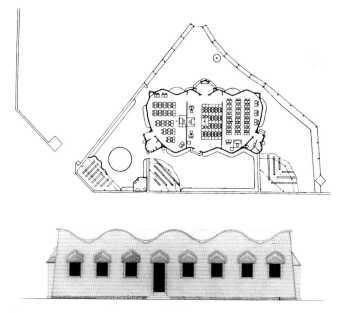

General plan and rear elevation.

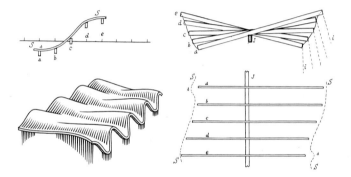

Wavy roof made of partitioned panel, drawing by Joan Bergós Massó.

The Sagrada Familia 1883-1926

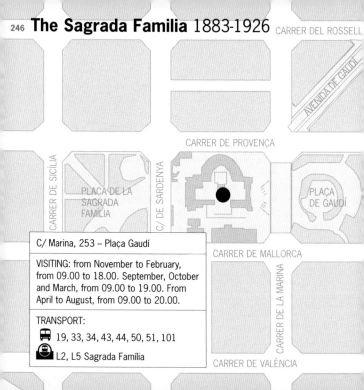

CARRER DEL ROSSELL

AVINGUDA DE GAUDÍ

CARRER DE PROVENÇA

CARRER DE SICÍLIA

C/ DE SARDENYA

PLAÇA DE LA SAGRADA FAMILIA

PLAÇA DE GAUDÍ

CARRER DE MALLORCA

CARRER DE LA MARINA

CARRER DE VALÈNCIA

C/ Marina, 253 – Plaça Gaudí

VISITING: from November to February, from 09.00 to 18.00. September, October and March, from 09.00 to 19.00. From April to August, from 09.00 to 20.00.

TRANSPORT:

🚌 19, 33, 34, 43, 44, 50, 51, 101

🚇 L2, L5 Sagrada Família

On the 3rd of October, 1883, at the age of 31, Gaudí accepted the commission to carry on the work of building Barcelona's new cathedral, begun by the architect Francisco de Paula Villar y Lozano, for which he was recommended by the architect Joan Martorell. Obviously, Gaudí had to combine his work on the project with the other works he undertook during his forty-three year professional career.

However, this was not so in the last twelve years of his life, as his poor health after 1910 meant he had to rest for long periods.

Before describing Gaudí's work on the cathedral, a brief description of the project as a whole is required. The Sagrada Familia (the Expiatory Temple of the Holy Family) is based on a Latin cross ground plan, consisting of five naves, an apse and a transept. The main nave and the transept are 95 and 60 metres long respectively. The central nave is 15 metres wide, the side naves are half this, and the transept is 30 metres wide.

Looking at the cathedral's ground plan allows us to see it should have three facades, facing east, south and west: the Nativity, Glory and Passion facades.

On the other, north-facing side is the apse, consisting of seven chapels with an ambulatory. Each of these facades is composed of ample porticoes, which are crowned in turn by four towers set in pairs to leave a central space for a sculptural element; the average height of these bell towers is 100 metres.

To mark the centre of the crossing, Gaudí designed an immense dome 170 metres high to be the symbol identifying the cathedral. In the project, the central nave was to be 45 metres high and the lateral naves 30 metres.

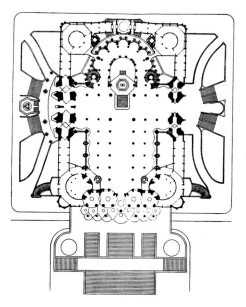

General plan.

Looking at the cross section, we can see that halfway up the lateral naves, Gaudí has included galleries for groups of singers.

Finally, note the idea of the perimeter cloister that Gaudí wanted to introduce, intending this space to act as a kind of buffer between the city and the interior of the cathedral.

Before describing the project as it stands, I would like to make an important point, namely that Gaudí took responsibility for continuing a building whose size meant he was unlikely to see it completed. Leaving aside this point, which has more to do with means and dedication, Gaudí greatly changed the project (without actually demolishing any of what had already been built), completely transforming Villar's neo-Gothic ideas for the cathedral. Gaudí went beyond Viollet-le-Duc's theories, not only accepting the construction as a reconstruction and attempting to make it perfect, but going one step further and responding to the imperative need to develop beyond a style which is undoubtedly lacking in secrets, and in which his involvement would have been practically anonymous, as is the case for so many other cathedrals and churches.

His studies of the structural behaviour of Gothic architecture led Gaudí to believe it could be simplified, adopting new approaches that would lead to a more daring, innovative design. He dispensed with lateral buttresses, using the tiered galleries on the inside for this purpose. This solution means the side facades are relatively sheer, and this means the slightly recessed bell towers on each facade make the whole composition more vertical.

Gaudí had to wait until 1900 to see part of the interior facade of the Nativity facade raised into place. Here we find nothing but geometry and architecture.

General view of the temple in 1933.

The vision, in its entirety as well as in detail, is a progress through a multitude of stone volumes differing greatly is size and shape. It is essential to know how to understand this vision composed of fragments. It is easy to be distracted by its monumental character, yet in contrast to the opposite face of the temple, it is here, in the attentive contemplation of this skeleton, that we can see a distinctive, unique manifestation of the evolution of Gaudí's work. The design of this facade was completed in 1917. Up until 1926, Gaudí was working on sketches for the chapel of the Assumption of the Virgin, situated in the perimeter cloister, for the sacristies on either side of the apse, new stained glass windows, and the structure of the vaults, as well as studies for the columns, in which Gaudí carried out an astonishing process of analysis and revision, transforming their outline by breaking down the geometry of the entire height of the column into individual pieces of the same diameter.

In 1915, Joan Rubió made a sketch of the temple complex as a whole in which the general dimensions can be appreciated.

When Gaudí died in 1926, the pinnacles of the four towers on the Nativity facade remained uncompleted, and his closest collaborators immediately finished them. After the hiatus of the Spanish Civil War (1936-1939), work on the temple was resumed, and it has intensified since 1980. This work is being performed by a multi-disciplinary team of technicians and craftsmen, and will be faithful to Gaudí's ideas. The cathedral will have the appearance Gaudí intended, but the means and construction techniques being used are very different from the ones Gaudí would have used. Obviously, changes in building regulations mean the project has to be very thoroughly monitored,

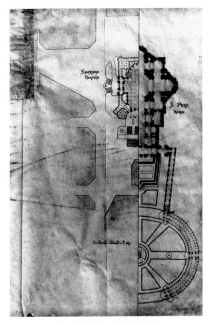

Scale sketch comparison with Saint Peter's in Rome.

but the work being performed seeks to be faithful to the designs produced by Gaudí and his collaborators.

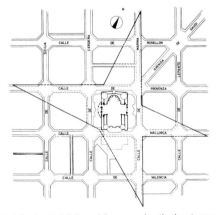

Site and sketch for best visibility, while occupying the least area.

Cross-section.

Sketch of the project drawn by Joan Rubió i Bellver in 1915.

View of the main nave during construction. ▶

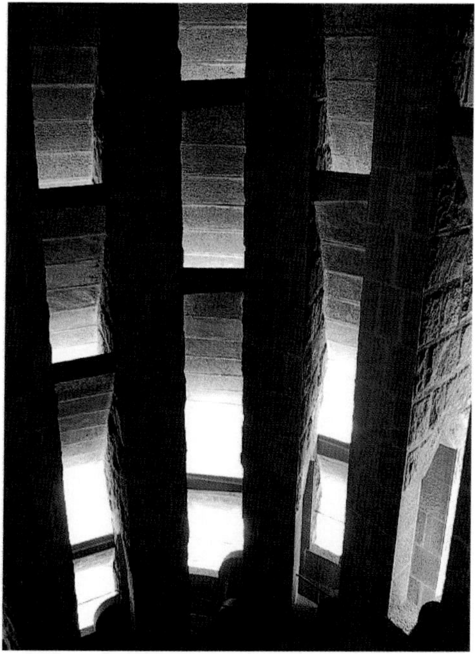

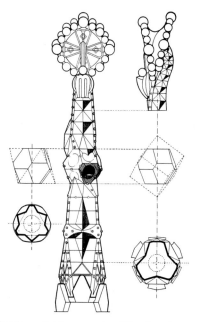

Elevations showing the underlying geometry of the pinnacles.

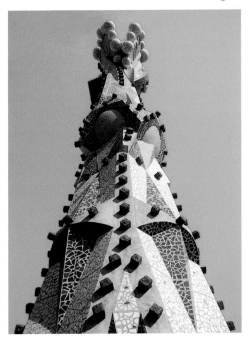

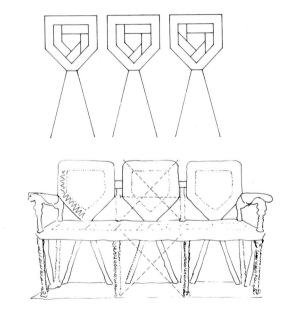

Bench for the officiating priests. Note the supports of the seat match each of the three backs.

Crypt for the Colonia Güell 1898-1908-1915

Santa Coloma de Cervelló
(Baix Llobregat, Barcelona)
Carretera de Sant Boi de Llobregat
a Sant Vicenç dels Horts

COLLABORATING ARCHITECTS:
Josep Canaleta and Francesc Berenguer

VISITING: Sundays from 10.00 to
13.00 (93 685 24 00).

TRANSPORT:

 Barcelona (Plaça Espanya)

 FFCC (train towards Santa Coloma,
alight at Molí Nou station)

L 70 Ciutat Cooperativa de Sant Boi

Gaudí was commissioned by Eusebi Güell in 1898 to build a church for the textile workers' colony (factory and housing estate) he owned. Over the next ten years, Gaudí produced countless studies and models of how to resolve the church's structure.

Gaudí wanted to arrive at a synthesis of all the forces in play in a building. He painstakingly analysed the structural behaviour of Gothic churches, but his aim was to move beyond Gothic by reducing the columns and buttresses, to find a single structural element capable of absorbing all the forces acting on it. He therefore reduced all of the component parts to create a unique form which, although inclined and geometrically unusual, provided him with a completely new solution for this building.

There are only a few sketches to show Gaudí's vision of the church as a whole, of which only the crypt was actually built.

This building is Gaudí's most expressive. The interior space, for example, can be considered as two areas, a central area including the altar, and a second area, a U-shaped ambulatory running around the perimeter.

In the central area, note the structure of the roof, supported by four leaning columns and a wall, recalling a main apse and its annexes, that together define this central area.

In the second area, which runs around the central area, we can see how a double circulation system is organised around the central crossing, which is reflected in the roof structure by a 180° turn. This does not, however, correspond to the way the crypt is used, since the whole of the interior functions as a single space. These two spaces we have described occupy approximately half of the plan.

Plan of the structure of the roof, drawing by Lluís Bonet.

The difference between the interior and exterior of this building is of considerable significance. The interior is intended to focus attention on a single point, the altar, but the exterior is harder to interpret, since the surrounding trees tend to camouflage and conceal what should be the base, the socle, of the building as a whole. The admirable treatment of the successive porticoes of the porch makes them seem a continuation of the rather random distribution of the trees.

The smooth texture and the colours of the roof of the porch suggest the canopy of a grove of trees. The eleven slanting columns making up this porch are all differently textured and treated, as if Gaudí wanted to create new species of tree to enrich the surrounding pinewood, and they form a perfect introduction to the space within. The different triangular areas to be seen on the roof of this portico, whose treatment is modulated by the use of a combination of glazed and matt ceramic elements, all of them set flush with the stonework, contrast with the buttresses and the outer skin of the crypt. The texture of the stone on the exterior, which almost seems to want to be hidden behind thick ivy, is crowned by openings recalling the shapes of parts of the human body. These openings contain the stained glass windows, whose varied geometrical forms almost always include a cross, and which bathe the interior in different colours of light as the sun moves across the sky. The air of mystery which the crypt might have as an empty building is transformed by the presence of the furniture, especially the small bench or pew, articulating the interior space.

The adjoining gardens contain the stone columns that were going to support the roof of the upper floor, lying full-length, like tombstones.

In the crypt for the Colonia Güell, Gaudí sums up all of his past efforts in an attempt to enter a personal dialogue with his work, while avoiding associations that might hinder his work. He rejects the temptation to rely on established canons, seeking instead a thoroughly expressive architecture, and the final result is undeniably a remarkable success, despite being his most daring work, and the one for which he received total and absolute recognition.

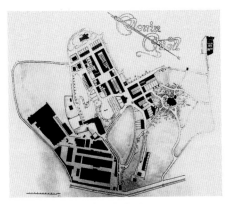

General plan of the Colonia Güell.

Model for studying loads and strains.
A replica can be seen in the Espai Gaudí in Milá House. ▶

Sections.

Wooden bench for two people, made of oak and wrought iron.
Note the arrangement of the seat in an arch.

Works built outside Barcelona

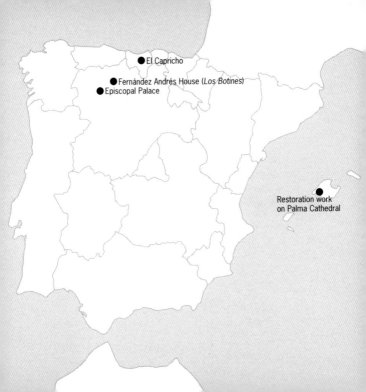

● El Capricho

● Fernández Andrés House (*Los Botines*)

● Episcopal Palace

● Restoration work
on Palma Cathedral

El Capricho 1883-1885

This summer villa for Máximo Díaz de Quijano, adjacent to the palace of the Marquis of Comillas, was built at the same time as the Vicens House and is a response to the same stylistic influences. It has a quite different programme, however, consisting of a half-basement, a main floor and an attic under the roof. The entrance, located at one corner of the house, is clearly identified by the tall cylindrical tower made of brick and clad in glazed ceramic tiles. The base of the tower takes the form of a porch with four columns, while the upper part is crowned by a belvedere. This tower is the most striking feature of the whole composition. Gaudí also produced an interesting corner belvedere element, giving free rein to his creativity in his treatment of benches that also constitute the railings, but here the decorative effect is smoother and more uniform than in the Vicens House. The simultaneous use of courses of hand-made brick and strips of glazed ceramic tile with a distinctive relief completes the house's exterior. Here, the windows are set flush with the plane of the facade, with a very pronounced vertical division, while the inside can be used as a belvedere.

The on-site supervision and direction of the construction work was carried out by Cristobal Cascante and Camil Oliveras, fellow students of Gaudí's at the Barcelona School of Architecture.

Comillas, Santander
VISITING: restaurant open 10.30 to 23.30 every day (94 272 03 65)

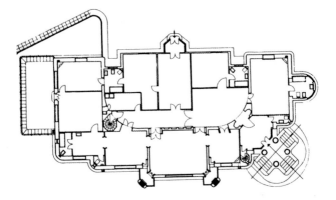

Episcopal Palace 1887-1893

After the destruction by fire of the original bishop's see, Gaudí received the commission to construct the new palace.

The building consists of a basement, ground floor, main floor and attic.

All of the exterior walls that make up the building's various facades are in grey granite, while in the interior Gaudí used load-bearing walls, pillars with capitals and cross-vaulting, as well as ogival arches.

With the exception of the main entrance, which has a portico with two flared arches, the rest of the building shows great unity of composition. The various turrets emphasize the vertical nature of the walls and give the building's exterior great continuity, adopting a neo-Mediaeval style in the treatment of the corners. The force thus conferred on the mass of stone gives the work as a whole an excessively overpowering effect.

Unfortunately, Gaudí did not himself finish the building. When the archbishop who commissioned him died, Gaudí declined to supervise the construction work. Thus the Episcopal Palace in Astorga can only be partly attributed to Antoni Gaudí. This fact makes itself fully apparent to the observer, even though those people who completed the project made every effort to follow Gaudí's plans.

Astorga (León)

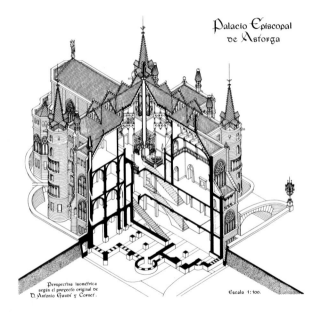

Palacio Episcopal de Astorga

Perspectiva Isométrica
según el proyecto original de
D. Antonio Gaudí y Cornet.

Escala 1:100.

Axonometry according to the original design.

Fernández Andrés House 1891-1894

This free-standing building built by Gaudí in the historic centre of the city of León is a good illustration of the period of doubt and uncertainty Gaudí was living. Here we can see how he has refined the neo-Gothic style he had already used in earlier schemes.

When he designed this building, Gaudí said he was familiar with the place in which it was to stand. Nevertheless, the project to a large extent ignores its surroundings, including a number of important buildings, and introduces a previously unknown architectural style into León. The way in which the masonry is handled, the clearly French influence of the cylindrical bay windows, and its excessive size, all mean this building does not fit in with its context. However, this is made up for by the way the scheme is resolved. For example, the ground floor has a structure with cylindrical pillars fanning out at the top, and which fits in perfectly with the building's finish, creating an ambulatory around the outer skin of the building, a formal device which Gaudí was to utilise to masterly effect in Park Güell.

The other floors were intended for use as living quarters, and are built in factory-produced brick and follow precisely the same layout as the ground floor. The facades, where the geminate windows of the first floor are combined with other, smaller, windows, are crowned by the volume of the slate roof, and dormer windows as vertical as the corners. The strips of flashing that run around the entire building clarify to some extent the functional division within.

Los Botines
Plaza del Obispo Marcelo, León

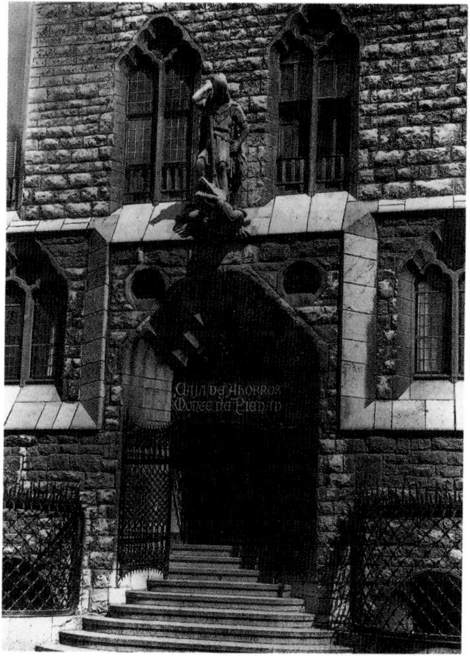

Restoration work on Palma Cathedral 1903-1914

Gaudí's contribution to this building ought to be considered in two parts. The first was limited to reorganising the internal functional layout of the cathedral, by shifting the choir to the presbytery and bringing the altar forward. The second, and more important, intervention can be divided into four parts: Jujol's decoration of the choir stall with paintings and carvings based on plant forms, the baldachin-chandelier, the pulpit and the stained glass windows.

Jujol's decorative painting deserves our admiration, and though it is a lesser work its use of colour is exceptionally powerful. These polychrome fragments painted on the boards of the 15th century choir stall undoubtedly deserve our fullest attention, and we should condemn the negative judgement they received in their day, incomprehension that led to their destruction. The decorative work on the wall alongside the choir, with its incrustations of glazed plant stems and leaves and auxiliary elements, is also excellent.

The baldachin-chandelier, the most potent piece in the entire intervention, is still the model built for Gaudí and Jujol. This is best seen from the door in the main facade. The framing of the image of the Virgin and the subtle suspension of this great chandelier are admirable.

Palma de Mallorca
COLLABORATING ARCHITECTS: Joan Rubió i Bellver and Josep Maria Jujol
VISITING: open at times of worship

Biography

1852 Born in Reus, Tarragona, on the 25th of June. Son of
Francesc Gaudí i Serra and Antonia Cornet i Bertran.

1863 to 1868 Attends the Pious School in Reus.

1873 to 1878 Studies at the Barcelona Provincial School of Architecture.

1875 to 1877 Works in the studio of the architect Francesc de Paula
del Villar y Lozano.

1876 Works alongside Josep Serramalera on various projects and as a
draughtsman for the industrial machinery manufacturers Padrós
i Borrás.

1877 to 1882 Collaborates with the master builder Josep Fontseré.

1878 Is awarded his professional qualification as an architect (March 5th).
Descriptive memorandum on the project for the laying out of plazas
and boulevards in the city of Barcelona (June). Manuscript on
Ornamentation (August 10th). Makes the acquaintance of
Eusebi Güell, his future patron and sponsor.
Wins a municipal competition with the sketch design of the lampposts
which now stand in the Plaça Reial in Barcelona. Over the next ten years
Gaudí takes part in the trips organised by the Association of Architects
of Catalonia and the nationalist Catalan Association for Scientific
Excursions, which was particularly interested in the study of Catalan
antiquities and architecture. In 1883 he saw Viollet-le-Duc's 1849
restoration of the walled precinct of Carcassonne.

1881 Takes part in the competition for the construction of a sailing club in
San Sebastian, without winning any of the prizes.

On the 2nd and 4th of February, the *La Renaixença* magazine publishes his article on "Exhibition of the Decorative Arts" in the Institut del Foment del Treball in Barcelona.

The general site plan of the Cooperativa Obrera Mataronense (Mataró Workers' Co-operative), incorporating his first ideas, is published.

1882 Supports Joan Martorell in the controversy over the project for the facade of Barcelona Cathedral. Eusebi Güell purchases an elevation drawing of the Martorell project, with lettering by Lluis Domenech i Montaner and drawn by Gaudí, subsequently reproduced in La Renaixença in February 1887. This drawing is now preserved in the Historic Archive of the Architects' Association of Catalonia.

Monsignor Collell, Dr. Torres i Bages and Antoni Gaudí.
Dr. Torres i Bages, Gaudí's father and his sister-in-law.
Dr. Torres i Bages y Antoni Gaudí.

1883 On the recommendation of Joan Martorell, Gaudí is appointed to take over from Francesc de Paula del Villar y Lozano as architect in charge of the Sagrada Familia in Barcelona.

1887 Travels in Andalusia and Morocco in company with the 2nd marquis of Comillas.

1904 The Calvet House receives the first of the prizes awarded by Barcelona City Council for the best building in the city.

1906 Takes up residence in the house designed by Berenguer in Park Güell, although the last years of his life were spent entirely in his studio-cum-living quarters beside the Sagrada Familia.

1908 Gaudí is asked to carry out a study for a hotel in New York City, of which a sketch by Joan Matamala has survived to the present day

1910 Exhibition devoted to Gaudí's work in the Société Nationale des Beaux Arts in Paris. This is to be the only exhibition on Gaudí's work held outside Spain during his lifetime. As a result of his grave illness Gaudí is obliged to retire from public life. The following year, accompanied by his physician Pedro Santaló, he moves to Puigcerdà, Girona.

1914 Death of Francesc Berenguer Mestres, architect and close friend of Gaudí's. From this time on, Gaudí's sole concern is with continuing his work on the Sagrada Familia.

1918 Death of Eusebi Güell (August 8th).

1922 For the first time an official body, the Congress of Architects of Spain, pays homage to Gaudí's work.

1926 Gaudí is knocked down by a tramcar on the corner of the Gran Via de les Corts Catalanes and carrer Bailén, in Barcelona (June 7th). Three days later he dies, in the Hospital de la Santa Cruz, and is buried in the crypt of the Sagrada Familia.

Dr. Torres i Bages and Antoni Gaudí.
Dr. Eusebi Güell, Gaudí and Dr. Torras i Bages

Chronology of works and projects

1867 First drawings for the Reus magazine "El Arlequín".

1867–1870 In collaboration with Josep Ribera and Eduard Toda, he works out a scheme for the restoration of the monastery of Poblet (Tarragona). His project report, the Memorandum on the Restoration of Poblet Monastery, should not be overlooked.

1875–1876 Project for the Spanish Pavilion for the Philadelphia Centenary Exposition.

1876 Student project: Courtyard for the Barcelona Provincial Council. Project for an academic competition: a pier.

1877 Project for a monumental fountain for the Plaça de Catalunya in Barcelona. Project for a General Hospital for Barcelona. Final project: a main hall for a university.

1877–1882 Collaborates with Josep Fontseré, master builder, on the project for the Parc de la Ciutadella.

1878 Scheme for lampposts for the Plaça Reial (inaugurated in September 1879).
Sketch design for the Vicens House.
Glass display case to show gloves by Esteban Comella, for the Universal Exposition in Paris.

1878–1882 Project for the Cooperativa Textil Obrera Matoronense in Mataró. Design for a kiosk for Enrique Girosi.

1879 Decor for the Gibert pharmacy at 4, Passeig de Gràcia, in Barcelona (demolished in 1895).

1880 Scheme for the electric lighting of the Muralla de Mar, in collaboration with Josep Serramalera.

1882 Project for a hunting pavilion for Eusebi Güell in Garraf, Barcelona.

1883 Altar design for the chapel of the Holy Sacrament in the parish church of Alella, Barcelona.

1883–1888 House for the tile manufacturer Manuel Vicens in carrer Sant Gervasi, now 24-26, carrer de Les Carolines. In 1925–1926, the architect Joan Baptista Serra Martinez widens a corridor of the house, and the walls and the boundary of the plot are changed. Gaudí is notified of the conversion.

1883–1885 House for Máximo Díaz de Quijano, "El Capricho", in Comillas, Santander. Site supervision of the project under construction is carried out by Cristobal Cascante, a former fellow-student of Gaudí's.

1884–1887 Gatehouses for the Güell estate: gatehouse and stables on the Avinguda de Pedralbes in Barcelona, now home to the Cátedra Gaudí (Chair of Gaudí Studies, inaugurated in 1953) of the Escola Técnica Superior de Arquitectura de Barcelona.

1884–1926 The Sagrada Familia.

1886–1889 The Güell Palace, a townhouse for Eusebi Güell and his family at 3-5, carrer Nou de la Rambla. Since 1954 this building has housed the Barcelona Theatre Museum.

1887 Design for a pavilion for the Compañia Transatlántica for the Exposición Naval in Cádiz.

1887–1894 Episcopal Palace in Astorga, León. The commission comes from the bishop in person, a Reus man, His Excellency Joan Baptista Grau i Vallespinos. In September 1893, on the bishop's death, Gaudí resigns his post as supervising architect.

In 1894 the diocesan architect of León, Blanch y Pons, is proposed as his successor. Starts work on the Palacio Manuel Hernández y Álvarez Reyero in 1899. In 1914 construction of the exterior of the Palace is completed under the direction of the architect Ricardo Guereta. In 1936 the building is used as a military headquarters, offices for the Falange and temporary quarters for artillerymen. In 1960, the bishop, Dr. Castelltor, starts on the definitive installation of the episcopal see in the Palace, although his sudden death prevents the completion of this work. His successor, the bishop Dr. González Martín, gives the building a new role, housing the Museum of Highways, which it still houses today.

1888–1890 Teresian College at 41, carrer Ganduxer, Barcelona, to a commission by Enrique de Ossó, the Order's founder.

1891 Casa Fernández Andrés, the *Casa de Los Botines* in the Plaza de San Marcelo in León. Gaudí receives the commission from José y Aquilino Fernández Riu and Mariano Andrés Luna, acquaintances of Eusebi Güell.

1892–1893 Scheme for a building for the Spanish Franciscan Missions in Tangier.

1898–1904 Calvet House, at 48, carrer Casp, Barcelona. Although the building bears the date 1899, the work of decoration, including the well-known furniture, made by Casas and Bardés, is not completed until 1904.

1898–1915 Crypt for the Colonia Güell, in Santa Coloma de Cervelló, Barcelona. Although the work is started in 1908,

it does not begin in earnest until 1912. The church was consecrated
on the 3rd of November, 1915. Work on site is supervised
by Gaudí's friend and assistant Francesc Berenguer.

1900–1902 Torre "Bellesguard", for Jaume Figueras, at 16-20,
carrer Bellesguard, Barcelona. Joan Rubio i Bellver collaborates
on the direction of work on site. In order to save the ruins of
what was once the palace of King Martin the Humane,
Gaudí constructs a viaduct in 1908.

1900–1914 Park Güell, on the Muntanya Pelada, for Eusebi Güell,
with the collaboration of Josep Maria Jujol.

1901–1902 Wall and gate for the estate of Hermenegild Miralles,
in the Passeig de Manuel Girona.

1901–1902 Refurbishment of the marquis de Castelldosrius' house,
carrer Mendizábal 19 (now carrer Nova Junta de Comerç), Barcelona.

1902 At the request of Ricard Company, contributes to the decoration
of the (no longer extant) Café Torino, at 18, Passeig de Gràcia,
Barcelona, alongside Pere Falqués, Lluís Domenech i Montaner and
Josep Puig i Cadafalch.

1903–1914 Restoration of the Cathedral of Ciutat de Mallorca, commissioned
by the bishop. Pere Campins. Francesc Berenguer, Joan Rubio i
Bellver and Jujol also participate.

1904 Scheme for a house for Lluís Graner.

1904–1906 Conversion of the Batlló House. Josep Maria Jujol
also contributes to the scheme.

1906–1910 Milà House "La Pedrera", at 92, Passeig de Gràcia, Barcelona, for Rosario Segimon de Milà. Josep Maria Jujol participates in the project. In 1954, Francisco Javier Barba Corsini converts the attic into studio-apartments, adding a number of elements to the terrace.

1909–1910 Schoolrooms for the Sagrada Família.

1912 Pulpits for the parish church in Blanes, Girona.

1923 Studies for the chapel of the Colonia Calvet in Torelló, Barcelona.

1924 Pulpit for a church in Valencia.

Bibliography

The bibliography on Antoni Gaudí is exceptionally extensive. The first important bibliography appeared in J. F. Rafols Fontanals and Francesc Folguera's *Gaudí*, Editorial Canosa, Barcelona, 1929. This gives a comprehensive catalogue of books and articles published up to that date.

In 1973, George R. Collins, with the support of the American Association of Bibliographers, published *Antoni Gaudí and the Catalan Movement, 1870-1930*, The University Press of Virginia. The bibliography covers the complete range of publications on Gaudí and Catalan Art Nouveau (Modernisme) up to 1970, approximately.

There has been no lessening of interest in the work of Gaudí since the latter volume appeared. I would, nevertheless, like to mention:

Bassegoda Nonell, Juan, *Antoni Gaudí i Cornet*, Edicions Nou Art Thor, Barcelona, 1978.

Bassegoda Nonell, Juan, *Guia de Gaudí*, Edicions Nou Art Thor, Barcelona, 1988.

Bergós Massó, Juan, *Gaudí, el hombre y la obra*, Universidad Politécnica, de Barcelona, 1974.

Codinachs, Macià (ed.), *Artículos manuscritos, conversaciones y dibujos de Antoni Gaudí*, Colegio Oficial de Aparejadores, Murcia, 1982.

Dalisi, Riccardo, *Gaudí, mobili e oggetti*, Electa Editrice, Milán, 1979.

Flores, Carlos, *Gaudí, Jujol y el Modernismo catalán*, Aguilar, SA de Ediciones, Madrid, 1982.

Güell, Xavier, *Antoni Gaudí*, Editorial Gustavo Gili, Barcelona, 1987.

Hitchcock, Henry-Russell, *Gaudí*, a catalogue of the exhibition held
at the MOMA, New York, 1957.

Lahuerta, Juan José, *Antoni Gaudí, 1852-1926. Arquitectura, ideología
y política*, Electa España, Madrid, 1993.

Le Corbusier, J. Gomis y J. Prats, *Gaudí*, Editorial RM, Barcelona, 1958.

Martinell, César, *Gaudí, Su vida, su teoría, su obra*, Colegio de Arquitectos
de Cataluña y Baleares, Comisión de Cultura, Barcelona, 1967.

Pane, Roberto, *Antonio Gaudí*, Edizione di Comunità, Milán, 1982.

Quetglas, José, "A. Gaudí i J. M. Jujol a la Seu", en D'A, Col.legi Oficial
d'Arquitectes de Balears, Palma de Mallorca, hivern 1989, pp. 40-71.

Sert, Josep Lluís, y James Johnson Sweeney, *Antoni Gaudí*, Ediciones Infinito,
Buenos Aires, 1969.

Solà-Morales, Ignasi de, *Gaudí*, Ediciones Polígrafa, Barcelona, 1983.

Solà-Morales, Ignasi de, *Eclecticismo y vanguardia. El caso de
la Arquitectura*, Editorial Gustavo Gili, Barcelona, 1980.

Tarragó, Salvador (ed.), *Antoni Gaudí*. Ediciones del Serbal, Barcelona, 1991.

Technische Hogeschool Delft, *Gaudí. Rationalism met perfecte materiaal
Beheersing*, Universitare Press, Delft, 1979.

Sources of the illustrations

Cátedra Gaudí; Frédéric Géraud; Antoni Gonzáles; Xavier Güell; Ediciones Doyma SA; Rafael Vargas (p. 203); Arxiu Documentació Gràfica, Biblioteca ETSAB; Arxiu Històric, COAC; Arxiu Mas; Bonet i Baltà, Museu del vi, Vilafranca del Penedés. (drawings pp. 325 and 327).

Alvar Aalto, with Sostres, Balcells, Pratmarsó and Moragas, 1954.

Some drawings and illustrations come from the following books and magazines:

César Martinell, *Gaudí, Su vida, su teoría, su obra*, Colegio de Arquitectos de Cataluña y Baleares, Comisión de Cultura, Barcelona, 1967.
Arxiu de Documentació Gràfica de la Biblioteca de l'ETSAB, *Gaudí.* Drawn by the students of ETSAB, Barcelona, 1985.
Riccardo Dalisi, *Gaudí, mobili e oggetti*, Electa Editrice, Milán, 1979.
Asociación de Arquitectos de Cataluña, Anuario (yearbook), 1913 and 1916.
Arquitectura y Construcción, Barcelona, 1917.
Panorama Nacional, tomo segundo, Hermenegildo Miralles, Editor, Barcelona, 1898.
CAU, numbers 69 and 70.
J. F. Ràfols y Francesc Folguera, *Antonio Gaudí*, Editorial Canosa, Barcelona, 1929.
Cuadernos de Arquitectura, no 20, Diciembre 1954.

About the author

Xavier Güell Guix, was born in 1950 in Barcelona, and graduated as an architect from the Escuela Técnica Superior de Arquitectura de Barcelona, ETSAB, in 1977. He has an office in Barcelona and since 1997 he has been a lecturer at the La Salle School of Architecture, Barcelona.